School Exclusion

School Exclusion

Research Themes and Issues

Isabelle Brodie

David Berridge

UNIVERSITY
UP *of* **JL**
LUTON PRESS

British Library Cataloguing in Publication Data
A catalogue record for this book is available from the British Library

ISBN: 1 86020 013 3

Published by
The University of Luton Press
Faculty of Humanities
University of Luton
75 Castle Street
Luton
Bedfordshire LU1 3AJ
United Kingdom

Telephone: +44 (0) 1582 743297; Fax: +44 (0) 1582 743298
e-mail: ann.simmonds@luton.ac.uk

Contents

School Exclusion

Introduction

The exclusion of pupils from school has become a matter of considerable interest in recent years. Not only has there been a significant rise in the number of exclusions taking place, consequently attracting much media attention, but the area is also one which has been subject to a number of developments in policy. The issue is a complex one which spans a range of educational and social factors, and this is reflected in the nature of the research into exclusion which has been undertaken.

This report is based on an invited seminar held at the University of Luton and funded by the Department for Education and Employment which sought to provide a forum for discussion between researchers and policy makers on the subject of school exclusion. More specifically, three objectives were identified:

- to exchange information and ideas between researchers with a common interest in school exclusion

- to promote dialogue between researchers and representatives of central and local government with responsibility in this area

- to discuss research findings in areas of policy interest.

The seminar brought together a wide range of individuals, 23 in all, with an interest in the issue of exclusion (see Appendix A). Researchers included representatives from both academic institutions and voluntary organisations throughout Britain. Individuals were also present from the Departments of Education and Employment, Health and Home Office, local government and the Commission for Racial Equality.

Academic interests were equally diverse, encompassing research into exclusion at both primary and secondary school level in England and Scotland, studies of specific groups of excluded pupils and their families, and research into issues which are closely intertwined with exclusion, such as special educational needs and inter-agency working. In view of the complexity of the issue, such wide-ranging contributions were found to be helpful.

1

The seminar took place over two days and consisted of a series of presentations by researchers and local government representatives interspersed with discussion. Summaries of research projects and the seminar programme are included in Appendix B. The report which follows is not a step-by-step account of the proceedings of the seminar, but seeks to identify the authors' view of the key themes which emerged as significant, together with the suggestions made regarding the direction which research in this area may take. The issues raised by those with responsibility for policy in this area, and the relationship of these to research, will also be examined.

Research background

Children have always been suspended and expelled from school, and a number of previous research studies have examined the phenomenon (Galloway *et al*, 1982; McManus, 1987; McLean, 1987). Such research continues to form an important base for current studies. However, interest in the issue has greatly increased in recent years, mainly as a result of the rapid increase in the numbers of children being expelled or 'excluded' from school during the late 1980s and 1990s.

This has taken place alongside a change in the law which replaced the more familiar terms 'suspension' and 'expulsion' with that of 'exclusion'. The Education (No 2) Act 1986 made provision for three types of exclusion: fixed-term, indefinite and permanent. This changed with the introduction of the Education Act 1993 in September 1994, which abolished the category of indefinite exclusion and limited fixed-term exclusion to 15 days in one term. It is important, therefore, that distinctions are made between the different forms of exclusion. In addition, it should be noted that local education authorities have somewhat different duties in regard to voluntary aided schools. In May 1994 Circular 10/94 was issued (Department for Education, 1994). This guidance aimed to clarify exclusion procedures within schools and offered guidelines on factors to consider when looking at exclusion. It emphasised that this should be a last resort measure taken in response to serious acts of misbehaviour.

Discussion at the seminar confirmed that research interest in exclusion has increased and this has performed an important function both in alerting policy makers to the rise in the numbers of exclusions taking place and seeking to explain this trend. However, in many respects this research is still relatively limited. This is partly no doubt due to the sensitivity of the issue and difficulties in obtaining reliable information. It has also tended to develop in a somewhat fragmented fashion – hence the importance of the seminar in examining the current state of research in this area.

The sudden nature of the rise in exclusion has led researchers to concentrate on particular aspects of the problem. Probably inevitably, interest has focused on questions of 'who', 'why' and 'how many'. In each of these areas of research some clear trends can be identified.

The early 1990s saw a variety of surveys by a range of organisations, including the media and professional groups, which aimed to measure the numbers of exclusions taking place (for example, Advisory Centre for Education, 1992; National Union of Teachers, 1992; Secondary Heads Association, 1992; MORI, 1993; National Association of Head Teachers, 1994; Office For Standards in Education, quoted in the *Times Educational Supplement* 28.10.94; the *Independent* 15.6.95). The National Exclusions Reporting System (NERS), set up by the Department for Education, reported in 1993 an increase in the number of permanent exclusions from 2,910 in 1990-91 to 3,833 in 1991-92 (Department for Education, 1993). Since then research has demonstrated a continuing rise, with the number of permanent exclusions passing 11,000 in 1993-94 (Hayden, 1994; Department for Education, 1995). While there have been significant differences in the methods of data collection adopted in these surveys, the dramatic increase in the number of exclusions, specifically permanent exclusions, taking place at both primary and secondary school level is undeniable.

Certain groups of pupils have been identified as being especially vulnerable to exclusion from school. Gender is highly significant, with boys three to four times more likely to be excluded than girls. Children from minority ethnic groups, in particular African-Caribbean males, are also excluded in disproportionate numbers. A further group experiencing high levels of exclusion are children looked after by local authorities ('in care'). The factor uniting these latter two groups is a high level of social disadvantage. This coheres with a long-standing tradition of social and educational research linking such disadvantage with low educational achievement and behavioural difficulties at school, which policy has sought to address (see, for example, Douglas, 1964; Rutter *et al*, 1979).

It is important to locate the growth in exclusions within the context of concerns expressed throughout the 1980s at an apparent rise in the occurrence of difficult and disruptive behaviour in schools. However, tensions exist with certain changes in education policy which, researchers have argued, lead to conditions within schools which might make exclusion more likely to be adopted as a sanction. The introduction of Local Management of Schools (LMS) has been viewed as significant (Lovey, Docking and Evans, 1993; Blyth and Milner, 1993). Some researchers also claimed that current law regarding exclusion affords pupils insufficient protection and that the situation was rendered problematic by the fact that Circular 10/94, as with all circulars, is advisory only. This lack of protection was felt to be particularly evident in regard to appeals procedures. However, while these explanations are important, there is little research evidence that schools readily exclude pupils; indeed for many head teachers and teachers, exclusion is a traumatic event which they work hard to avoid.

Researchers had also identified much variety in the development of exclusion policy and procedure between local authorities. Some were considerably further ahead than others and it was argued that, in the light of the seriousness of the issue, policy might generally have been expected to develop more quickly. The diversity of policy seemed to be even greater in Scotland, where of course an alternative education and legal framework operates. Differences in policy were related to the fact that, while south of the border the powers of local education authorities have been significantly curtailed, in Scotland these have largely been retained. This diversity within Scotland was reflected in a number of areas. There were, first of all, considerable differences in the volume of policy documents issued by departments. This suggested that varying degrees of significance were attached to the issue. Some policies also formed part of a broader youth policy. However, while this on occasion appeared impressive, individuals to whom such information would have been relevant were not always aware of such strategies.

Policy at both national and local level can influence the way in which exclusion takes place throughout a country. The continuing variations in local policy specifically are a matter of concern. It was also felt that some impending developments in local authority government, notably local authority reorganisation in 1996, may have important implications for the development of exclusion policy in both England and Scotland.

Data on exclusion

For both policy makers and researchers, an understanding of the extent of exclusion and identification of those most at risk is in large part dependent on the amount and nature of official data. Researchers at the seminar were in agreement that the number of exclusions has increased and is increasing, with some making reference to this rise as 'inexorable' and 'relentless'. However, major concerns were expressed regarding the data held by local authorities about exclusion.

These concerns are related both to the different types of information and statistics which local authorities collect and their methods of recording. Notably, researchers had also frequently found information on exclusion to be poorly stored and maintained. Attention was drawn to three areas of specific concern.

Firstly, we must consider information regarding the numbers of exclusions taking place. It was noted at the seminar that data may not distinguish between the number of exclusion *incidents* and the number of *children* to which these incidents apply. Therefore, five fixed-term exclusions may be recorded without reference to the fact that these have applied to one child.

Secondly, an area of considerable difficulty relates to the distinction made between informal or unofficial exclusion and exclusion where official procedures are followed. While informal exclusion may cover a wide range of circumstances and an acceptable definition is hard to find, it was agreed that failure to take account of this phenomenon led to a situation in which official statistics could underestimate the scale on which exclusions were taking place. This issue is even more complex within the Scottish context, where the lack of an overarching legal framework regarding exclusion has led to considerable differences in what kinds of exclusion existed and/or were permitted in different authorities. Therefore, while informal exclusion was explicitly forbidden or permitted in some authorities, it was not acknowledged in others.

A further concern emerged about the failure of some local authorities to collect basic data on excluded children. An example was provided of one authority where no reason for exclusion was recorded. Such omissions are obviously serious in terms of ascertaining whether an exclusion is justified and, consequently, if it should be upheld. It was also reported that information regarding the ethnicity of excluded pupils was frequently absent or incomplete. This deficiency is especially worrying in view of the evidence which exists demonstrating the disproportionate numbers of African-Caribbean males excluded from school (Bourne, Bridges and Searle, 1994) and, in turn, undoubtedly exacerbates the difficulties of research in this area.

Perhaps the most important issue researchers felt should be addressed was the variability reported in the way in which local authorities collected and recorded data on exclusion. This was also borne out by the recent Department for Education survey, which found that, for example, 29 LEAs had a computer database on which they recorded details of all pupils out of school, 11 were in the process of producing such a database while the remaining 38 used manual systems (Department for Education, 1995). This finding had emerged in both English and Scottish research and has some worrying implications both for accessibility to data and for the overall efficiency of the system . This fact is somewhat alarming given the apparent evidence that local authorities and individual schools vary greatly in their exclusion rates. Unless comparable information is available, such measurement must be cautiously undertaken. Notwithstanding this fact, it appears that even taking account of problems relating to data, differences continue to exist in exclusion rates between local authorities with, for example, significantly higher exclusion rates in the London boroughs compared to those for other areas. It was also noted that very little is known about variations in exclusion rates between different types of school, for example in grant-maintained or voluntary aided schools.

It is clear, then, that local authorities are at very different stages in their collation of information regarding school exclusion. This may be related to the level of policy development. It is therefore extremely important that researchers acknowledge these differences when publishing exclusion statistics if a more accurate understanding of the pattern of exclusions is to be achieved.

Excluded pupils

Excluded pupils share a number of characteristics, in terms of such factors as gender and family background. However, it was emphasised that while understanding of these common factors is extremely important, this should not lead to a perception of excluded pupils as an entirely homogeneous group. Indeed, the problems which these young people displayed were often highly individual in nature and their family backgrounds exceedingly complex.

Nevertheless, areas of overlap can be identified. As has already been noted, the majority of excluded pupils are male, with boys about four times more likely to be excluded than girls. This was reflected in research samples: for example in some studies using intensive case study methods, no cases of girls had been forthcoming. All research findings related to excluded pupils emphasise the considerable disadvantage which these pupils have generally experienced.

High levels of family stress, including unemployment, low income and family disruption are evident. This is reflected in the disproportionate number of pupils who are excluded and who are also looked after by the local authority. However, many families of those excluded had experienced contact with a range of outside agencies. Both the young people and their families, therefore, typically presented multiple needs.

The majority of pupils, as might be expected, are excluded at secondary school level and in particular at Years 10 and 11 (14 to 16 year olds). A variety of reasons have been mooted for this including, for example, the view that the sometimes lengthy Statementing process for pupils with emotional and behavioural difficulties – a problem for pupils of all ages – is even less likely to be undertaken when pupils are close to school leaving age. Among the reasons given for exclusion, disruptive and aggressive behaviours are prominent. However, research consistently indicates that, for the majority of young people, exclusion appears to take place following a steady build-up of tension rather than any dramatic incident. In some instances, though, a serious infraction of school policy, for example regarding drugs, will trigger the exclusion – what one researcher described as the 'big bang' exclusion. The link between school exclusion and delinquent behaviour outside the school is a matter of considerable importance (Home Office, 1995). The relationship is a complex one and further research is undoubtedly required.

Primary school pupils

Differences among excluded pupils are particularly apparent between the primary and secondary school groups. As we have noted, the number of primary school exclusions has increased and it is important that the nature of the exclusions taking place among younger children are understood when considering making appropriate responses to the problem.

As with excluded pupils generally, gender and ethnicity are significant among the younger group. Boys are even more likely to be excluded in junior school than in secondary, with one study finding boys to be nine times more likely to be excluded (Hayden, 1995). African-Caribbean boys are especially at risk of exclusion. The majority of younger children excluded have also been identified as having special educational needs.

The circumstances of the primary school children excluded would appear, if anything, to be even more complex and traumatic than their older peers. Many children had experienced some form of family disruption and a large number had been looked after by the local authority. Large proportions of families had no member in paid work. Substance misuse and involvement with the courts for a wide range of offences were also common. In a high number of cases there were also experiences of disability or bereavement in the family. Unsurprisingly, then, the primary school children studied exhibited high stress ratings and, inevitably, most had very low self-esteem.

Exclusion from school is typically associated with behavioural difficulties. On a behaviour rating scale high levels of conduct disorder, hyperactivity and restless and disorganised behaviour have been identified among this group. Significantly, the wide range of needs presented by these children was recognised by teachers and they were rarely seen as 'plain naughty'. However, where reasons were recorded for a child's exclusion, physical aggression appeared to be especially prominent among the younger group.

One research study had constructed a model of risk factors relating to personal, family and school characteristics which increased the child's vulnerability to exclusion. Where these different factors interact the risk of exclusion is, inevitably, considerably heightened. Some issues emerged here which can easily be overlooked: for example the significance of a child's size – where a child was very small or noticeably larger than other children, this could be a factor in their exclusion or at least in the way they were perceived by teachers. An understanding of the risk factors which render a child vulnerable to exclusion is clearly crucial if effective intervention is to be made possible. While the realisation that a child exhibits a large number of risk factors may, as the researcher pointed out, raise the spectre of the 'nightmare scenario', it can also offer the opportunity to plan for the child's educational welfare and social integration.

Another area of difference between the situation of pupils excluded at primary school level compared to those of secondary school age may be that of parental involvement. While it is probably true for excluded pupils of all ages that there are more positive outcomes where parents are especially proactive, it was suggested that parents can exert greater influence where their children are at primary school. In one study, interesting differences were observed to exist between an affluent sub-group of parents and the majority who were less affluent. The former group were more likely to locate the problems within the child and to seek the diagnosis of a problem which could then be treated. Those parents who were less affluent, on the other hand, were more willing to consider the child's difficulties within the wider context of family circumstances and, consequently, to entertain the idea of different types of intervention. This was attributed to the more frequent contact these families had experienced with a wide range of agencies.

Exclusion is a serious and highly traumatic event for children; one seminar participant said that the effects were worse than having a criminal record. For those of primary school age, there is clearly a danger that delay in finding alternative education or reintegration into mainstream schooling may have serious long-term effects on the child's subsequent educational welfare.

Ethnicity

The ethnicity of excluded pupils is a matter of considerable importance, but it is also an area in which research has made an insufficient contribution. This is partially due to the lack of reliable data. It also results from the geographical areas in which research has taken place, some of which have very small minority ethnic populations which do not emerge in sample groups. Consequently, the Scottish research, for example, was unable to examine the issue in detail.

Previous research, mostly locally based, has consistently identified a disproportionate number of exclusions among African-Caribbean males. A 1991 study in Nottingham, for example, found that African-Caribbean pupils were five times more likely than their white peers to be excluded (Bourne, Bridges and Searle, 1994). In some cases the decision to exclude has been identified as discriminatory. In such cases the reasons for exclusion have included religious or cultural 'non-conformity', the failure to recognise cultural elements in incidents which occur within the school, and the misdiagnosis or disregard for medical or educational problems specific to an ethnic group.

Researchers at the seminar were agreed that African-Caribbean males continued to be disproportionately represented among excluded pupils. In one local authority studied, the proportion of African-Caribbean boys of junior school age excluded was three to four times their proportion in the population. Notably, one study of primary school age pupils had also found that children from other minority ethnic groups were under-represented. The reasons for such under-representation are also a matter for further research.

Hard evidence which provides an explanation for the over-representation of African-Caribbean males in exclusion statistics is difficult, if not impossible, to find. In discussion of this issue it was suggested that one avenue of investigation relates to the way in which teachers perceive African-Caribbean pupils in the classroom – in terms of appearance and other culturally linked forms of behaviour. In regard to the primary school group it was suggested that where a child was large for his age and was also African-Caribbean, this has been perceived by some teachers as potentially threatening. Clearly this is discriminatory and raises important training needs.

Alternative educational provision

When children are permanently excluded from school or indeed are not attending school for other reasons, LEAs are required to make some form of alternative provision for these pupils. The nature of such provision is crucial as an intervention in the educational career of a pupil with behavioural difficulties. It is therefore important to assess the subsequent educational careers of excluded pupils, though in this we are hampered by a lack of longitudinal and comparative research.

Educational provision for excluded pupils may take a variety of forms, most commonly home tuition or Pupil Referral Units (PRUs). The adequacy of such provision has frequently been questioned, especially in the light of the fact that it is typically part-time. A recent OFSTED (1995) inspection of 12 PRUs concluded that while the relationships between pupils and teachers in the units were good and the behaviour and attendance of pupils often improved as a result of smaller groups and increased pupil/teacher interaction, standards of attainment were generally low.

In accordance with the OFSTED report, researchers reported significant differences in the patterns of subsequent educational provision made for excluded primary and secondary school pupils. A range of types of provision existed. Home tuition services continue to provide for a high proportion of pupils from both groups, on average for approximately five hours per week. A wider range of services were available to older pupils including, for example, joint packages with social services and further education colleges. Also, significantly more young people of secondary school age attend PRUs than those excluded from primary schools. In some areas, the local authority contracted out to other organisations such as Cities in Schools. Where this occurred the costs were not found to be significantly greater. Researchers noted that in some areas creative and innovative work was being carried out but perceived resource constraints made this difficult for others.

A variety of problems were identified concerning the actual arrangements for excluded pupils. Delays in finding placements are frequent, and can militate against reintegration in the longer term. The amount of education offered these pupils is very limited, sometimes involving as few as two sessions each week. Although such provision fulfils the legal obligations of the local authority, this also increases the difficulty of reintegration to mainstream school as well as leaving children unoccupied for long periods of time. At present available data suggests that approximately 27 per cent of all excluded primary age pupils and 15 per cent of secondary pupils return to mainstream, though this is probably an underestimate (Department for Education, 1995). Significantly, researchers were in agreement that children themselves were, virtually without exception, anxious to return to school, regardless of age and reason for exclusion. In some cases the quality of education provided in special units was also criticised, while acknowledging that teachers are often working in quite difficult circumstances. Inevitably such services have been placed under pressure by the increase in the numbers of permanent exclusions.

Children with special educational needs (SEN)

Children with special educational needs have consistently been identified as being among those most at risk of exclusion. The term 'special educational need' is a broad one, and the group with which we are most concerned regarding exclusion is that of children with emotional and behavioural difficulties ('EBD').

The increased incidence of exclusion among pupils with SEN is a worrying trend, suggesting a shift away from the philosophy of integration of such pupils into mainstream schools. Notably, however, an increase in the number of exclusions from special schools has also been reported. A variety of factors have been suggested by researchers as influential in leading to this situation, including lower tolerance on the part of schools in dealing with pupils with behavioural problems, and reduced access to support services as schools become increasingly responsible for the management of their own budgets (see, for example, Bennathan, 1992). However, it was acknowledged at the seminar that there is a lack of hard evidence in this area and the relationship between SEN and exclusion is undoubtedly a complex one. Difficulties in the Statementing process do appear to be significant. This may involve delays in this process or, in the case of older pupils, an unwillingness on the part of schools to consider extra support on the grounds that these pupils will shortly be leaving school. It is important that the relationship between exclusion and special educational need should continue to be examined following the introduction of the 1994 Code of Practice on the Identification and Assessment of Special Educational Need (Department for Education, 1994). This provides a valuable framework for assessment procedures and, though these must of course be supported by adequate resources, it may have a significant role to play regarding exclusion.

Concerning the primary school group, researchers had found a major over-representation of pupils with SEN among excluded pupils. Nearly all the children studied were already Statemented for EBD or moderate learning difficulties ('MLD'), or were in the process of formal Statementing, at the time of exclusion. This was sometimes perceived by other professionals as an attempt by the school to obtain resources. Certainly some schools did feel that exclusion, while by no means desirable and not undertaken lightly, could strengthen their claim for extra support for a child.

Interestingly, this group was not seen as having major learning difficulties and were mostly considered to be of average ability. It was pointed out that this may be a matter of perception; teachers in particular tending to feel more able to deal with learning rather than behavioural difficulties. Here the effects of a child displaying extremely disruptive behaviour on other pupils should also be taken into account.

When examining the issue of SEN, the way in which and by whom such need is defined is a matter of immense importance. This is a theoretical problem which nevertheless has practical implications for the way in which interventions take place. Indeed, our understanding of this may well have significance for our perception of exclusion. As it was pointed out, the very idea of EBD is both value-laden and context-specific. It is therefore unsurprising that rates of EBD, as with exclusion, will vary among schools.

It was argued that the distinction between pupils labelled as EBD and pupils perceived as 'disruptive' was often unclear and sometimes meaningless. As with most such labels, it is subject to negotiation between relevant individuals. The label must also be legitimised and it was argued that this takes place through a definition of the child's behaviour as being in some sense irrational and involving emotional disturbance, together with the belief that the child was inappropriately placed in mainstream school. It was suggested that the child with EBD was in fact perceived to be *qualitatively* different to other pupils.

Discussion of this issue highlighted the fact that exclusion can take place through a variety of processes. The child who is assessed as having emotional and behavioural difficulties and is moved to a special school is also, in one sense, 'excluded'. While this may in some cases be a course of action which is in the best interests of the child, it is important to examine whether this is in fact the case or whether such action simply legitimises the failure of teachers to change the young person's behaviour. Exclusion may operate in a similar manner. It should be noted that, in contrast, where teachers identified pupils as 'disruptive' they usually felt able to maintain the child in the school. Here perceptions of the resources available may also play a significant part. However, resource issues do not necessarily dominate in the process leading to assessment of a child being identified as having emotional and behavioural difficulties. It was also pointed out that the perceived effects of the child on other children in the group are important in this respect.

Children looked after by local authorities

Children looked after by the local authority represent another group which is especially vulnerable to exclusion. This is not a new phenomenon. Earlier studies of exclusion also highlighted this fact; for example in Galloway's (1982) research, half of the excluded young people in the sample studied had been in the care of the local authority at some time. In 1992, research by Stirling revealed the high level of exclusion among children living in residential accommodation, and also demonstrated the considerable proportion of this group which was *informally* excluded. In the studies of exclusion represented at the seminar, extremely high levels of contact between social services and children who were excluded were identified. The significance of this group emerged in all the research studies examined, and therefore merits separate discussion.

The type of contact children who are excluded and their families will have with social services will vary considerably, and the issue should be examined in the context of changes which have taken place in the pattern of children's services and since the introduction of the Children Act 1989. At the present time approximately 50,000 children are looked after by local authorities in England, including just over 32,000 in foster care and about 8,000 in residential accommodation. Others will have contact with social services through, for example, family centres (Department of Health, 1994). In Scotland the most recent figures show almost 12,700 children in public care, the vast majority – over 80 per cent – in some form of community based non-residential accommodation (Scottish Office, 1994).

The overlap between children looked after by social services and those who are excluded from school is unsurprising. The disadvantage and family stress which has been identified as common among children who are excluded also of course represent the factors which are likely to lead to social services' involvement (Bebbington and Miles, 1989).

It has been argued, however, that being looked after by social services further disadvantages a child educationally. Research has suggested that education is not prioritised in social work planning and that schooling is disrupted by frequent changes of placement (Fletcher-Campbell and Hall, 1990). In regard to residential care, the educational environment of a children's home tends not to be conducive to encouraging educational achievement (Jackson, 1987; 1989). Young people and residential staff also sometimes feel that children looked after are stigmatised in the educational system. Circular 10/94 suggested that children living in children's homes could be more likely to be excluded on the grounds that they had access to full day time supervision. This view does not in fact seem to be supported by the emerging evidence. Research at the

11

University of Luton is showing that the number of children living in children's homes who are permanently excluded is usually quite small – they are often not attending for other reasons. Furthermore, teachers do not appear to view these children as a homogeneous or discrete group, accepting that they may have educational difficulties but not seeing this as inevitable.

All the research studies represented at the seminar reported high levels of social services involvement with children excluded from school. Many children appeared to experience a large number of changes in placement. This was the case for both younger and older children and in England as well as Scotland. Young people not only changed foster or residential placement, but also their place of education. In one study three-fifths of the sample of adolescents had experienced a change in school for reasons unrelated to age.

One study focusing on children looked after in residential accommodation reported that residential staff and social workers tended to be poorly informed regarding education and in some cases the former were unsure whether a young person had in fact been officially excluded. Contacts between social workers, residential homes and schools were frequently very poor, and when problems emerged the response tended to be reactive rather than proactive. In common with other forms of inter-agency working, roles tended to be poorly defined and squabbles between education and social services regarding funding were common. However, some interesting parallels between the views expressed by the different groups involved in the exclusion process were reported. In one study head teachers and social workers emerged as having similar perceptions of the needs of children, whereas the views of residential key workers were more akin to those of parents.

It is important to emphasise that the educational difficulties to be found among children looked after by local authorities do not begin at entry into the residential home or to foster care. Regarding residential care, it is clear that many children are already excluded or have indeed experienced more than one exclusion at the time of entry. Social workers, however, are sometimes pessimistic and believe that a residential placement will increase the likelihood of exclusion in the case of a young person whose educational placement is already tenuous. Unfortunately we have little research evidence regarding the pattern of exclusion in foster care; this is an area which would undoubtedly benefit from further research attention.

One positive development regarding children looked after, which is intended to heighten awareness of the significance of education, is the Looking After Children initiative developed by the Department of Health (Ward, 1995). Education is one of the priority areas where children's needs are identified. Appropriate action is planned in response to these needs and responsibility allocated to specific individuals to carry this out. This initiative clearly has considerable potential to address some of the problems discussed above. However, the development of positive relationships between children's homes, fieldworkers, schools and other agencies should also have high priority in meeting the educational needs of this group of young people.

School processes

Central to an understanding of the reasons why exclusion takes place must be examination of the behaviours which lead to exclusion and the way in which these are perceived and defined by teachers and other professionals. There is a strong body of educational research which has examined the significance of what is termed 'the school effect' (for example, Mortimore *et al*, 1988; Reynolds and Cuttance, 1992). In other words, outcomes for individual pupils displaying similar behavioural difficulties, and indeed educational outcomes more generally, can vary considerably depending on the school which they attend. However, the constellation of factors on which the school effect depends is complex, and it should not be assumed that the alteration of any single area of school policy or practice will automatically lead to a dramatic change in outcomes.

In regard to school policy, it appeared from the research conducted that exclusion could be related in a variety of ways to a school's wider discipline policy, and could have a significant impact on the way exclusion was managed. There is, again, considerable diversity in such policies. This seemed to be particularly noticeable at primary school level; researchers reported that in some schools fixed-term exclusion represented a quite routine part of the discipline policy but formed no part in others. It was agreed that, generally, schools did not evaluate the effects of their policies on exclusion – for example in relation to the subsequent educational career of a young person – and that when a pupil was excluded on a permanent basis this usually involved a total break in the relationship.

It was acknowledged at the seminar that schools are required to balance a number of interests when considering the retention or exclusion of a pupil. This task is by no means easy. Head teachers must take account of the needs of the individual child, but also of the views of other children in the class, parents and teaching staff. This fact affects both the decision to exclude and the subsequent relationships between schools and other agencies. In addition, there are implications for research, which in examining exclusion should also investigate school and classroom dynamics.

However, the interests of these different groups are liable to conflict. In a context where policy has emphasised the importance of parental choice, schools must take into consideration the views of other parents. It was suggested that, on the whole, the 'silent majority' of parents tend to support exclusion as a policy. Certainly in some cases schools felt that pressure from other parents had represented the final straw when making the decision to exclude a child. Situations were reported where other children had been significantly upset by the difficult behaviour of one child, who is also likely to demand substantial amounts of a teacher's attention. It was pointed out that the action of excluding one child may fulfil a function other than that of protecting the interests of other children. In particular, it was suggested that exclusion of a child could represent a means of communicating acceptable standards of behaviour to the rest of a class or a school. On the whole, researchers agreed that teachers are often under considerable pressure when dealing with a child whose behaviour was especially difficult or disruptive. The necessity of implementing a very structured curriculum was highlighted as a constraint, and it is unclear how the needs of young people with emotional and behavioural difficulties can best be met within this context.

Account should also be taken of relationships which exist within the educational system. It was pointed out that the idea of inter-agency working encompasses not only liaison between different services but also between the different levels of schooling and between the school and the local authority. Thus, it is important that good relationships are developed between nursery and primary schools, and also between the primary and secondary sectors. The way in which transitions between different stages of schooling are managed may be very important for the subsequent social and academic progress of the young person.

The issue of the relationship between the school and the local education authority is especially important in view of the increased independence of the school from the LEA. Management of this relationship can be a sensitive matter. Tensions can, for example, emerge over the admission to another school of pupils who have previously been excluded. More generally, it was reported that schools frequently do not feel supported by LEAs in a number of areas. Not only do they consider that the resources available for dealing with pupils who present extreme behavioural problems are inadequate, but that exclusion procedures are unnecessarily complex. Nor is there sufficient encouragement for the exploration of in-school alternatives to exclusion.

Schools are engaged in a range of complex relationships which significantly affect their stance towards exclusion. Importantly, it was agreed that schools do not on the whole exclude readily and for many the process of excluding a child had been a very traumatic one. The nature of the involvement of other agencies was frequently significant; where this was especially proactive it appeared that schools' tolerance levels had been increased. The amount of information provided to schools when a child with behavioural difficulties was first admitted was also perceived to be an important factor, and an area where improved practice could be facilitated. It was also agreed that, if priority is to be given to maintaining children within mainstream schools, then they must have access to support both in terms of resources and expertise.

Inter-agency liaison

Given the range of needs which excluded children present, it was unsurprising to find researchers at the seminar reporting that a large number of agencies could be involved with the young person and his or her family. These ranged from social services and police to psychiatric services and family centres. The nature of the relationships between different services and the effectiveness of interventions carried out by several agencies working together undoubtedly represented one of the most prominent themes of the seminar.

Both child welfare and educational policy have emphasised the importance of effective working partnerships between services in meeting the needs of children. The Children Act 1989 places a duty on LEAs and district health authorities to provide services which are deemed necessary for children identified as being 'in need' (Section 27). Similarly, the Education Act 1993 requires social services and health authorities to comply with requests from the LEA in regard to children with special educational needs (Section 166). This latter point is further emphasised in the Code of Practice on Special Educational Needs (Department for Education, 1994). This states that given the range of difficulties which children with special educational needs may manifest, it is unlikely that educational objectives can be achieved without partnership not only between different services but also with parents and pupils. However, there are clearly many difficulties in implementing such partnership. The Audit Commission has noted that while parents and health, education and social services shared a common concern for the well-being of children, only in a very small number of local authorities had effective inter-agency working been developed (Audit Commission, 1994).

This would certainly appear to be the case for children excluded from school. Researchers agreed that, while some very effective work was being carried out in some local authorities, this was very piecemeal. Concern was raised that work with excluded pupils tended to take the form of crisis management rather than preventative strategies. Again it is clear that some interesting and creative schemes are being implemented in different parts of Britain but where these exist they tend to be very small in relation to the level of need. Obtaining resources for such schemes is also problematic, though GEST (Grants for Education Support and Training) funding had made a significant contribution in some areas.

Some positive initiatives were reported. These included, for example, a local authority where a social worker was employed to carry out a variety of preventive interventions with children experiencing difficulties. These included counselling, anger management and visits to the young person's home. This had proved effective in encouraging schools to maintain children. Work with the young person's family is very important and an account was given of another project where attempts were being made to establish a home/school liaison worker. It was noted here that having an individual who is independent of the school situation is important.

A number of specific areas of difficulty were identified. First of all, while it is obviously desirable that different agencies co-operate in relation to a child, and indeed are legally required to do so through the provisions of the Children Act 1989, it is also important that one agency has lead responsibility for the child's welfare. Unless roles are clearly defined and responsibilities appropriately allocated, planning for and work with the child can easily become lost in a welter of inter-professional wrangling. In some cases, researchers had found that the efforts of different individuals to protect professional boundaries and status can dominate negotiation to the extent that the child is almost eliminated from the discussion. It was agreed that the role of some agencies, such as educational welfare, can be unclear and vary considerably among local authorities.

A second, and unsurprising, issue identified by researchers was that battles over resources for an excluded child are common. In particular, it is often uncertain which agency should have responsibility for payment. Traditional disagreement or even conflict between professionals, most prominently between social services and education, also hampers effective practice. A further dimension of this problem may be the lack of comprehensive policies directed at adolescents. This also tends to be reflected in practical initiatives; a recent study of parenting programmes (Smith and Pugh, 1995) has found that the majority of these are aimed at the parents of *young* children, and suggests that further attention should be given to identifying when parents need most support. In social work, coherent preventative services for adolescents are uncommon (Triseliotis *et al*, 1995). This is an area which warrants further attention, in view of the evidence of the stress which exists among the families of excluded children.

Considerable interest, therefore, was expressed in research reported at the seminar which has evaluated 'Youth Strategy' policies in Scottish regional authorities. These are specifically aimed at inter-agency working. Account should of course be taken of the different meaning which inter-agency work holds in Scotland by virtue of the Children's Hearing System. A brief explanation of this may be helpful. The Hearing System is non-judicial and operates through Panels composed of lay people. Young people are referred to the Panel by welfare or educational agencies, and decisions are then made for the welfare of the child. This may include, for example, the making of a residential or supervision requirement. The Panel also has responsibility to oversee and review the situation of young people subject to statutory orders. This is usually perceived as a positive structure which encourages participation and joint decision making, but some aspects of the Hearing System may in fact create quite specific difficulties for inter-agency collaboration. While schools can refer a child to the panel for a decision on their education – such referrals are based on non-attendance criteria – and educational input can have a significant effect on the decisions made at the Hearing, the agency which implements the decision of the Hearing and carries the associated costs is social services. Such arrangements clearly have the potential to create tensions. (For a fuller explanation of the relationship between the Hearing System and Education, see Shaffer, 1995.)

Youth Strategies function quite differently across Scotland and schools are not always aware of their existence. Research has discovered that some operate within the context of broader community development policies, while other strategies are more specifically directed at, for example, preventing entry to residential care. In one authority a five-level process of inter-agency work was described. In this case the effectiveness of the strategy depended on the level of the hierarchy at which inter-agency work was taking place. It had been found that, as the process moved up the hierarchy, the more difficult it became to implement effective inter-agency practice, until at director level it became almost impossible. Difficulties were usually related to resource issues. On the whole, however, it was felt that Youth Strategies were working relatively well. Comparable programmes are seldom encountered in England.

Overall it was agreed at the seminar that the development of improved inter-agency working is a matter of urgency, both in relation to children who are at risk of exclusion and those who have been excluded. Without this, it was warned, it is likely that further services, such as the police, become involved in turn leading to the escalation of costs. However, the identification of strategies which can enable effective co-operation is far from easy. It is notable, however, that where good practice does seem to exist in regard to exclusion, inter-agency collaboration is invariably an important part of this.

It was pointed out that the development of local authority Children's Service Plans, mandatory from 1996, are potentially of considerable importance in the development of good practice in multi-agency planning and service provision. These aim to produce co-ordinated services for children. However, Children's Service Plans also reflect some of the problems discussed above. The Department of Health Social Services Inspectorate (1995) reported that, in local authorities where work on plans had begun, the mapping of need was most successful where particular types of need could easily be identified and where responsibility rested clearly with a lead agency. Where needs cut across more than one agency, measuring the extent of need and planning appropriate responses became much more difficult. This was due to the absence of, for example, information systems which provided information based on a wider definition of need and suitable decision making structures. Given that children excluded from school present just such a range of problems, this illustrates the complexity confronting Children's Service Plans.

Partnership with parents has also been an important element in recent policy. This principle is firmly embedded in the Children Act 1989 and is also a significant element in the Code of Practice on Special Educational Needs. It is also relevant to the Children (Scotland) Act 1995. Other educational legislation emphasises the importance of parental involvement in schools in a more general sense. Previous research has found that schools' perceptions of parents may be more negative where parents have little involvement in and show little outward support for the educational process.

It has been found that families tend to be uninformed about exclusion procedures, and may not have access to support or advocacy in making an appeal. Where a child is permanently excluded, the family is likely to experience considerable stress – often in addition to many existing problems. It was noted, however, that families typically wanted their child to be helped, to have friends and to become reintegrated into the life of the school. This is an important finding, which demonstrates the shared interest between parents and professionals in working for the best interests of the child. However, if the welfare of the child is to be promoted, inter-agency working may be required to meet the needs of the family as well as those of the individual child.

Resources

The question of the 'cost' of exclusion is complex and one of which it was generally agreed that research had taken insufficient account. Only one research study, it seems, has to date examined this in any detail (Parsons *et al*, 1994). However, this is an important issue and one which emerges as a source of tension in the management of all stages of the exclusion process. For schools, the resource issue arises when considering whether to exclude a child and researchers reported that staffing levels, availability of specialised support services and even the amount of physical space available could affect the head teacher's decision to exclude. The issue of resources may also have a more indirect influence on the processes associated with exclusion as well as with the actual decision to exclude. It was argued, for example, that even the definition of a child as having emotional and behavioural difficulties may depend on perceptions of the amount of resources available to meet such needs. This is especially pertinent in cases where arguments are being put forward for particularly expensive provision, such as residential schools. It would appear, therefore, that not only are the economics of exclusion important, but also the perceptions of those individuals with decision making powers regarding this group of pupils.

When a child is permanently excluded the school automatically loses the funding allocated to that pupil. This demonstrates the seriousness of informal exclusions where a child may not be attending school but still has a place on the roll, with the school retaining funding. However, the complexity of the situations of most children following exclusion may mean that resources freed up are not necessarily passed on. Costs are frequently borne by other agencies and these can be considerable. In the one study where costing was undertaken, it was found that provision for an excluded primary school pupil could cost three times as much as provision within school (Parsons *et al*, 1994). However it was pointed out that if the attempt is made to maintain a pupil in school, considerable costs will still be incurred, as children with severe emotional and behavioural difficulties require extra resources. The costs of different types of provision should therefore be carefully assessed.

While the issue of cost is important and should be carefully examined, it should not dominate discussion of exclusion. As it was pointed out, what is at stake is the welfare of the individual child. It was suggested that the conflicts which frequently arise over the allocation of funds for excluded children are due in part to the lack of sympathy with which they are viewed. However, in examining this issue, there is little doubt that debate is hampered not only by the lack of research examining costs *per se*, but also longitudinal research examining the outcomes for children who have been excluded and, consequently, the most cost effective ways of helping those children.

Research and policy

Dissemination of research findings emerged as a major item during the seminar. This is an important issue in view of the aim of the meeting to facilitate communication between researchers and those involved in different levels of policy development.

Some difficulties appeared to exist; these are not however specific to the area of exclusion and are common to the research/policy relationship (Dartington

Social Research Unit, 1993). Those involved in developing policy noted that accessible research findings were not always available. This is a thorny issue. It would seem that researchers must continue to seek imaginative ways by which the results of their research can be effectively communicated. These could include use of the press and other media. It was noted that several organisations, such as the National Children's Bureau, and some government departments produce helpful research summaries which can be utilised in the dissemination process (see, for example, Department of Health, 1995). DFEE sponsorship of this seminar was also felt to be a very positive step. In addition, it is important that research is directed at the different levels of policy making, and that findings do in fact reach those with responsibility for decision making.

It was pointed out that researchers in academic institutions are subject to a number of constraints regarding the ways in which findings are published. The current emphasis in higher education on publication in high status academic journals can militate against the interests of those seeking accessible research. Concern was also expressed at the ways in which media reports tend to over-simplify complex research studies. However, it is clearly important that dissemination should be close to the forefront in research design. Not only are researchers dependent on local authorities for access to research sites and hence have a responsibility to feed back their results, but effective communication is also essential if research is to have a positive impact on the policy process.

Directions for future research on school exclusion

While the possibilities for future research on exclusion in many respects seemed endless, some issues did emerge from discussions at the seminar as especially important. The attempt was also made to consider which aspects of exclusion had been given significant attention.

Mapping exclusion

This refers to an accurate understanding of exclusion generally – for example, how many children are being excluded, characteristics such as age, gender and ethnicity, the number of excluded children who are Statemented; and the way in which exclusion rates vary across local authorities. While the data on exclusion has improved considerably in recent years, it was felt that good quality data was only gradually emerging and work on this should continue. This process will be aided in future by the collection of statistics by the Department for Education and Employment which will include ethnicity and whether the excluded child is Statemented. However, another dimension of 'mapping' exclusion should also be longitudinal research, which examines the social and educational outcomes for children who are excluded. At present such research appears to be virtually non-existent. This would also be helpful in understanding the links between exclusion from school and involvement in criminal behaviour.

Characteristics of excluded pupils

The disproportionate number of African-Caribbean boys being excluded from school emerged as an area in which additional research is required. While the scale of this problem is clear, there are few adequate explanations for this phenomenon which are rooted in empirical research. Exploration of this issue may involve examination of wider school processes.

Many of the presentations during the seminar also indicated the complexity of the relationship between special educational needs and exclusion. While it is apparent that many children, especially those at primary school level, are Statemented or are in the process of being Statemented when they are excluded, the situation is less clear regarding those of secondary school age.

A further area which would benefit from future research relates to children looked after by local authorities who are excluded from school. Very little is known, for example, about the educational experience of children living in foster care. In view of the high level of social services' involvement with the families of excluded children, evaluation of the effectiveness of social work interventions in such cases would also be valuable.

Inter-agency working

It is clear that a wide range of agencies are likely to be involved throughout the exclusion process. Frequently, however, relationships between agencies and professionals could be significantly improved. Not only is it important that an understanding is reached of the way in which these relationships operate, but examples of good practice should also be explored and disseminated.

Costs

It was widely agreed that a more detailed understanding of the 'costs' of exclusion was necessary. Research in this area should cover not only the actual costs borne by other agencies as a result of a young person's exclusion, but also the cost of maintaining a child with difficulties in school, that is the cost of *inclusion*. Work currently being undertaken by the Audit Commission into troublesome young people more generally may be helpful here.

International comparisons

The meaning and implications of exclusion from school is a highly contested area. Policies have changed rapidly in recent years and continue to be subject to debate. However, the form which exclusion takes in a particular country is by no means inevitable, and examination of the responses made to difficult and disruptive pupils in other countries may be helpful in the development of both policy and practice. It was also noted that comparative research in the United Kingdom should have higher priority, particularly as this seminar has benefited from the dialogue between English and Scottish participants.

Conclusion

The seminar proved an important occasion for both researchers and policy makers to discuss and debate the many dimensions to the issue of exclusion from school. We would conclude that the initial aims of the seminar, namely to encourage communication between these two groups, relate research findings to policy interests and to encourage the exchange of ideas between researchers, were fulfilled. In addition some areas where further research regarding exclusion would be especially desirable were identified. It is important that such research should be multi-disciplinary in nature if the complex nature of the phenomenon of exclusion is to be fully appreciated. The links established through the seminar proved fruitful in developing understanding of the issue of school exclusion both academically and in terms of the implications for policy.

Bibliography

Abrams, F. and Ashton, K. (1995) 'Are Britain's schoolchildren more trouble than they used to be?', *The Independent*, 15 June.

Advisory Centre for Education (1992) 'Exclusions', *ACE Bulletin*, 45, 9-10.

Audit Commission (1994) *Seen But Not Heard – Co-ordinating Child Health and Social Services for Children in Need*. London: HMSO.

Bebbington, A. and Miles, J. (1989) 'The background of children who enter local authority care', *British Journal of Social Work*, 19, 5, 349-368.

Bennathan, M. (1992) 'The care and education of troubled children', *Therapeutic Care and Education*, 1, 1, 37-49.

Blyth, E. and Milner, J. (1993) 'Exclusion from school: a first step in exclusion from society?', *Children and Society*, 7, 3, 255-268.

Bourne, J., Bridges, L. and Searle, C. (1994) *Outcast England: How Schools Exclude Black Children*. London: Institute of Race Relations.

Dartington Social Research Unit (1993) *The Dissemination of Research Findings in Social Work*. Totnes: Dartington Social Research Unit.

Department of Health (1994) *Children Act Report 1993*. London: HMSO.

Department of Health (1995) *Children's Services Plans: An Analysis of Children's Services Plans 1993/94*. London: HMSO.

Department of Health (1995) *Child Protection: Messages From Research*. London: HMSO.

Department for Education (1993) A new deal for 'out of school' pupils. Press release, 126/93.

Department for Education and Department for Health (1994) *Pupils with Problems (DfE Circulars 8-13/94)*. London: Department for Education.

Department for Education (1994) *Code of Practice on the Identification and Assessment of Special Educational Needs*. London: Department for Education.

Department for Education (1995) *National Survey of Local Education Authorities' Policies and Procedures for the Identification of, and Provision for, Children Who Are Out of School by Reason of Exclusion or Otherwise*. London: Department for Education.

Douglas, J. (1964) *The Home and the School*. London: MacGibbon and Kee.

Fletcher-Campbell, F. and Hall, C. (1990) *Changing Schools? Changing People? The Education of Children in Care*. Slough: National Foundation for Educational Research.

21

Galloway, D., Ball, T., Blomfield, D. and Seyd, R. (1982) *Schools and Disruptive Pupils*. London and New York: Longman.

Hayden, C. (1994) 'Research into school exclusions', *Young Minds Newsletter*, 18, 13-14.

Hayden, C. (1995) *Primary School Children Excluded from School: Numbers, Characteristics, Reasons and Circumstances*. Paper presented at the European Conference on Educational Research, School of Education, University of Bath, 15-17 September.

Home Office Research Study 145 (1995) *Young People and Crime*. London: Home Office.

Jackson, S. (1987) *The Education of Children in Care*. University of Bristol: School of Applied Social Studies.

Jackson, S. (1989) 'Residential care and education', *Children and Society*, 2, 4, 335-350.

Lovey, J., Docking J. and Evans, R. (1993) *Exclusion from School: Provision For Disaffection at Key Stage 4*. London: David Fulton.

McLean, A. (1987) 'After the belt: school processes in low exclusion schools', *School Organisation*, 7, 3, 303-310.

McManus, M. (1987) 'Suspension and exclusion from high schools: the association with catchment and school variables', *School Organisation*, 7, 3, 261-271.

MORI (1993) Survey reported in 'A Class Apart', *Panorama*, BBC, 19 March.

Mortimore, P., Sammons, P., Stoll, L., Lewis, D. and Ecob, R. (1988) *School Matters – The Junior Years*. Wells: Open Books.

National Association of Head Teachers (1994) Dramatic Increase in Permanent Exclusion of Pupils. Press Release, 9 December.

National Union of Teachers (1992) *Survey on Pupil Exclusions*. London: National Union of Teachers.

Office for Standards in Education (1995) *Pupil Referral Units: The First Twelve Inspections*. London: HMSO.

Parsons, C., with Benns, L., Hailes, J. and Howlett, K. (1994) *Excluding Primary School Children*. London: Family Policy Studies Centre.

Reynolds, D. and Cuttance, P. (eds) (1992) *School Effectiveness – Research, Policy and Practice*. London: Cassell.

Rutter, M., Maugham, B., Mortimore, P. and Ouston, J. (1979) *Fifteen Thousand Hours*. London: Paul Chapman.

Secondary Heads Association (1992) *Excluded From School: A Survey of Suspensions from Secondary Schools in 1991-92*. Leicester: Secondary Heads Association.

Shaffer, M. (1992) 'The Children's Hearing System and education', in Lloyd, G. (ed) *Chosen with Care?* Edinburgh: Moray House Publications.

Smith, C. and Pugh, G. (1996) *A Survey of Group-Based Parenting Programmes*. Social Policy Research Findings 91. York: Joseph Rowntree Foundation.

Stirling, M. (1992) 'How many pupils are being excluded?', *British Journal of Special Education*, 19, 4, 128-130.

The Scottish Office (1994) *Statistical Bulletin (Social Work Series)*. Edinburgh: Scottish Office.

Times Educational Supplement (1994), no.4087, 28 Oct., p2.

Triseliotis, J., Borland, M., Hill, M. and Lambert, L. (1995) *Teenagers and the Social Work Services*. London: HMSO.

Ward, H. (1995) *Looking After Children: Research Into Practice*. London: HMSO.

APPENDIX A: List of Seminar Participants

Dr Derrick Armstrong	University of Sheffield
Roy Atkinson	Northamptonshire Education Department (Day 1)
Professor David Berridge	University of Luton
Dr Valerie Brasse	Department of Health
Lee Bridges	University of Warwick
Isabelle Brodie	University of Luton
Joe Charlesworth	Commission for Racial Equality
Jane Cocking	Department for Education and Employment (Day 1)
Wes Cuell	Bedfordshire Social Services
David Fraser	Bedfordshire Education Department
Dr John Graham	Home Office
Carol Hayden	University of Portsmouth
Dr Michael Hughes	Barnardo's
Brian Jones	Association of Metropolitan Authorities
Dr Andrew Kendrick	University of Dundee
Dr Kay Kinder	National Foundation for Educational Research
Professor Pamela Munn	Moray House Institute of Education, Edinburgh
Jonathan Owen	Association of County Councils (Day 2)
Dr Carl Parsons	Canterbury Christ Church College
Margaret Stirling	Underley Hall School, Kirkby Lonsdale
John Rowlands	Department of Health
Peter Thorpe	Department for Education and Employment
Peter Wilkinson	Department for Education and Employment (Day 2)

Professor David Galloway (University of Durham), Professor Jane Aldgate (University of Leicester) and Professor Mary John (University of Exeter) regrettably had to withdraw shortly before the seminar.

We are grateful to Professor Pamela Munn and Dr Carl Parsons for comments on an earlier draft of this report.

APPENDIX B: Seminar Programme and Summaries of Research Projects on School Exclusion

Thursday 8 February

12.30 – 1.30pm	Arrival at Putteridge Bury. Buffet lunch.
1.30 – 2.00	Introduction to seminar, background and objectives – David Berridge. Outline of programme and practical arrangements.
2.00 – 3.00	Presentations and discussion 1: Carl Parsons and Carol Hayden.
3.00 – 3.15	Tea.
3.15 – 4.15	Presentations and discussion 2: Pamela Munn and Derrick Armstrong.
4.15 – 5.45	Presentations and discussion 3: Michael Hughes, Andrew Kendrick and Isabelle Brodie.
7.30	Dinner. Informal discussion.

Friday 9 February

9.30 – 11.00am	Presentations and discussion 4: Lee Bridges, Margaret Stirling and Mary John.
11.00 – 11.15	Coffee.
11.15 – 12.15pm	Discussion of research themes and future research topics: introduced by Carl Parsons, Kay Kinder and Jane Aldgate.
12.15 – 1.15	Implications for policy and practice: introduced by ACC/AMA, Bedfordshire Education and Social Services representatives.
1.15	Lunch and depart.

Title of the research project:

NATIONAL SURVEY OF LOCAL EDUCATION AUTHORITIES' POLICIES AND PROCEDURES FOR THE IDENTIFICATION OF AND PROVISION FOR, CHILDREN WHO ARE OUT OF SCHOOL BY REASON OF EXCLUSION OR OTHERWISE

(Commissioned by the Department for Education)

Date started: January 1st 1995   **Completion date:** April 31st 1995

Researchers: Carl Parsons, Jean Hailes, Keith Howlett

Project aims:

The objectives of the investigation were to establish, for 109 Local Education Authorities in England, the following:

a.   In relation to policy and provision:

– LEA policies and general arrangements for the exceptional provision of education for pupils out of school;

– the stage of development of such policies;

– the management of education for pupils out of school including recording and monitoring arrangements, means of determining provision to be made for individual pupils and review procedures;

b.   In relation to permanently excluded school children:

– the total numbers excluded during the 1993/94 academic year from primary, secondary and special schools;

– the total numbers excluded in the period September 1st – December 31st from primary, secondary and special schools;

– the numbers experiencing the different forms of provision of education for permanently excluded pupils in the Autumn term of 1994: pupil referral units, home tuition and other means by which the LEA provide education otherwise than at school;

c.   In relation to the identification and illustration of good practice:

– selection of 4 LEAs to represent county and metropolitan types and distinctly different, successful or promising approaches to the provision of education for children excluded, or at risk of exclusion, from school.

Research design:

Directors of Education and Chief Education Officers were contacted giving information about the questionnaire which would arrive and asking for a contact person within the LEA who would be responsible for completing the questionnaire. The questionnaire was sent to all 109 LEAs in England and responses were eventually received from 101 LEAs allowing an accurate estimate to be made of the situation with regard to the development of policy, numbers of permanent exclusions and provisions made for excluded pupils.

Progress to date: The research is complete.

What has been learned, or learned to date if the project is still in progress?

1. Most LEAs have sought to revise policies to take account of the requirements of Section 298 of the Education Act 1993. Most LEAs have issued guidelines for head teachers and governors to clarify the new legal arrangements and almost all LEAs have some support arrangements to maintain behaviourally difficult pupils in school.

2. Almost a third of LEAs appear to have a computer database on which they record details of all pupils out of school.

3. Most LEAs have a panel to make decisions on placements of pupils out of school and in three quarters of the LEAs reviews take place half termly, or more frequently, of the provision for pupils out of school.

4. The total number of pupils permanently excluded from schools in 1993/94 estimated from 101 LEAs, was 11,181. The total number of recorded permanent exclusions in the Autumn term 1994, the term following the implementation of the 1993 Act, is 4,788.

5. In most LEAs the rate of exclusion appears to be increasing though in 26 of the 101 responding LEAs the rate of exclusion in the Autumn term 1994 appears to have fallen compared with the previous year. About 12% of permanent exclusions are from Primary school, 6% from Special school and 82% from Secondary school.

6. Exclusion rates in London LEAs are nearly twice those in metropolitan and county LEAs.

7. Provision for permanently excluded pupils in the Autumn Term 1994 indicates that, in the time-span of the survey, returns to the mainstream school occurs for under a quarter of the excluded pupils.

8. There are 238 PRUs in 101 LEAs catering for 212 Primary school pupils and 3,032 Secondary pupils. Home tuition caters for 338 Primary permanently school pupils and 2,122 Secondary pupils.

Publications/reports available:

National survey of Local Education Authorities' Policies and Procedures for the Identification of, and Provision for, Children who are out of school by Reason of Exclusion or otherwise. London: Department for Education, Pupils and Parents Branch.

Parsons, C. The Exclusion Zone. *Guardian:* July 11 1995

Parsons, C. and Howlett, K. *Difficult Dilemmas.* Education 186/25-26 December 1995.

Parsons, C. (forthcoming) *Permanent Exclusions from Schools in England in the 1990s: Trends, Causes and Responses.* Children and Society.

Parsons, C. and Howlett, K. (forthcoming) *Permanent Exclusions from School – A Case Where Society is Failing its Children.*

Name and address of person to contact for more information about this research:

Dr Carl Parsons, Reader in Education, Christ Church College, Canterbury, Kent, CT1 1QU. Tel: 01227 782351, Fax: 01227 470442, Email Address: c.parsons@cant.ac.uk

Title of the research project:
EXCLUDING PRIMARY SCHOOL CHILDREN
(Funded by the Joseph Rowntree Foundation)
Date started: April 1st 1993   **Completion date:** December 31st 1993
Researchers: Carl Parsons, Louise Benns, Jean Hailes, Keith Howlett

Project aims:
Through case studies of 11 children in 3 LEAs to:

- Describe events leading up to exclusion and the role of the school, parents and other agencies;

- Gather perceptions of the pupils' experiences of school from all implicated parties;

- Describe the child's experience whilst out of school, including the substitute educational provision;

- Assess the availability of support for the child and family during exclusion;

- Examine the legal framework within which decisions and actions take place with regard to the individual child;

- Estimate the costs of exclusion.

Research design:
The data gathering was carried out by means of semi-structured interviews with teachers, head teachers, school governors, social workers, educational psychologists and other professionals who were implicated in the 11 cases of permanent exclusion studied. Written permission was gained from the parents to approach other professionals involved in their child's exclusion or in the management of the case following exclusion. 82 individuals were interviewed and documentation was examined.

Progress to date: The project is complete.

What has been learned, or learned to date if the project is still in progress?
The main findings were:

- The majority of excluded primary school children come from families facing a range of problems. Over half of those studied were receiving support from social services;

- The average amount of schooling lost by the permanently excluded primary school children studied amounted to more than three quarters of a school year;

- Assessment procedures for children with emotional and behavioural difficulties are particularly slow and relatively ineffective in leading to proposed additional or alternative provision;

- The average delay in setting up home tuition was 14 weeks. The average amount of home tuition provided was 3 hours a week, compared with the standard 25 hour school week;

- Inter-agency co-operation to support the excluded child and the family is generally poor and provision of appropriate, integrated support for the child and his or her family rare;

- The cost of exclusion is high, with costs to the totality of other services greater than if the resources had been directed to maintaining the child in school;

- Greater support for both families and schools, and improved inter-agency working, are needed if disruption for individual children is to be minimised.

Publications/reports available:

Parsons, C. (1994) *Excluding primary school children*, London: Family Policy Studies Centre.

Parsons, C. (1996) 'The Cost of Primary School Exclusions', in *School Exclusions: Inter-Professional Issues for Policy and Practice*. Blyth, E. & Milner, J. (Eds) London: Routledge.

Name and address of person to contact for more information about this research:

Dr Carl Parsons, Reader in Education, Christ Church College, Canterbury, Kent, CT1 1QU. Tel: 01227 782351, Fax: 01227 470442, Email Address: c.parsons@cant.ac.uk

Title of the research project:
CHILDREN EXCLUDED FROM PRIMARY SCHOOL: POLICIES AND PRACTICES IN ENGLAND AND WALES (ref. ESRC Award no. R000234387)

Date started: September 1993   **Completion Date:** August 1995

Researcher(s): Carol Hayden, Carol Lupton, Brenda Lawrence, Christine Sheppard, Derek Ward.

Project aims and objectives:
(1) Identify key variables associated with primary school exclusions;

(2) Identify local authorities displaying a range of exclusion rates associated with key variables;

(3) Examine in depth the policies and practices of three local education authorities and schools within them, displaying a range of exclusion rates;

(4) Explore the experience of a small number of excluded children, and those of their parent(s)/carer(s), class and head teachers of the process of exclusion;

(5) Inform the development of alternatives to exclusions and support structures for primary schools.

Research Design:
(1) **National questionnaire**- investigating the numbers, characteristics, reasons and trends in primary school exclusion. Information obtained is for the 1992/93 academic year and the autumn term 1993.

(2) **Case studies of three LEAs** (a County Council and two inner London Boroughs) with contrasting policies and practices in relation to the support for children with behavioural difficulties, and such children when they are excluded from school. Documentary analysis of information on file about 265 primary age children excluded during the 1993-94 academic year, in these three LEAs. All types of exclusion were investigated. More limited fieldwork was carried out in an additional two LEAs (another County Council and inner London Borough), this work focused upon behaviour management strategies and behaviour support in primary schools in one LEA and the exclusion and under achievement of African-Caribbean children in the other LEA.

(3) **In-depth case studies of 38 excluded primary school children**. Parent(s)/carer(s), head and class teachers were interviewed and 22 of the children themselves

Publications/reports available:
Hayden, C., Sheppard, C. and Ward, D. (1996) *Primary Age Children Excluded from School.* SSRIU Report No. 33, University of Portsmouth.

Hayden, C. (1994) 'Primary age children excluded from school: 9 multi-agency tours', *Children and Society*, 9, 3, 257–273.

Hayden, C. (1995) 'Research into School exclusion', *Young Minds Newsletter*, 18, June, 13–14.

Progress to date:

Project completed. Report submitted to the ESRC December 1st 1995. Report will be in the public domain after the quality of the research has been assessed. However, the ESRC are willing for the main report to them and the summary to be circulated to participants at the seminar (8-9th February 1996).

Name and address of person to contact for more information about this research:

Carol Hayden, SSRIU (Social Services Research and Information Unit), University of Portsmouth, Halpern House, 1–2, Hampshire Terrace, Portsmouth, Hampshire PO1 2QF.

Tel: 01705 842800

Researcher's Summary – Carol Hayden

Exclusion from school is not a new phenomenon, although the terminology used has changed. Expulsion and suspension were more common terms until the Education Act 1986. Children have always been excluded from school and concerns about the management of exclusion have been evident for sometime (Lovey et al, 1993). Such concern prompted the government administered National Exclusions Reporting System (NERS), which monitored a two year period (1990/91; 1991/92) and reported in late 1992 (DfE, 1992). This study showed a rise in records of permanent exclusion over the two year period. Other surveys conducted at or around this time (such as the NUT, 1992, survey or the MORI, 1993 survey) produced wide-ranging estimates for all types of recorded exclusions.

Research and public interest was growing about the issue of exclusion at the time the ESRC project began (September 1993) but the evidence about what data were available and recorded in LEAs was patchy. Therefore the work began with a national survey both to gauge what information was available in LEAs and in order to make the research as representative as possible. This part of the research was funded from University resources. The original proposal was based on an expectation that the DfE survey data would be available in greater detail than they were. This expectation was not realised because of the DfE's concerns about the reliability of the data they collected.

The focus of the ESRC funded project was on the three main case study LEAs, 265 primary age children excluded from these LEAs in 1993-94 and 38 individual case studies of excluded children. The research investigated local authority management of and responses to primary school exclusion, as well as home and school based accounts of individual cases of exclusion. In so doing it produced the largest scale study to date of primary school exclusion, in terms of number of cases investigated. In its focus on the primary phase it is unusual in this field of research.

The research involved two main research methods (survey research and case study research) and a wide range of techniques, within a triangulation strategy. We are confident of the validity, reliability and representativeness of our research findings. The three main components of the research and the research findings are summarised in Figure 1.

Less detailed work has been conducted in a further two LEAs (again a County Council and an inner London Borough) which are in many ways comparable to those which form the basis of the more detailed case studies. Investigation in these two LEAs has followed up themes identified in the case study LEAs. The focus in the County Council is on policy in relation to provision and support for behaviour management in primary schools. In the inner London Borough a specific investigation was made into the exclusion of Black and minority ethnic pupils. This latter investigation was important in corroborating evidence in one of the other inner London Boroughs which recorded exclusion by ethnicity (the majority of LEAs did not do so).

Figure 1: overall research design

National information.	Literature review.
	Postal questionnaire all LEAs (England and Wales)(returns from 46 LEAs, 39% of total).
Case study LEAs (a county council and two inner London Boroughs).	Documentary analysis of policy and practice on exclusion and special educational needs provision. Collation of data on file of 265 excluded children: 134 in LEA 1; 99 in LEA2; 32 in LEA3.
	Interviews with key personnel in the education department and representatives of other agencies (social services departments, child and family guidance, voluntary agencies etc.). Over 50 interviews conducted.
Case studies of individual children (38 in total).	Child: booklet to accompany semi-structured interview, followed by discussion; observations made at the time of the visit.
	Parent(s)/carer(s): structured interview, completion of behaviour rating scale, followed by general discussion.
	Teachers (head and class teachers): postal questionnaire, documentary analysis of school policy on behaviour and discipline, structured interview, completion of behaviour rating scales, followed by general discussion.

Some key findings:

- An increase in recorded exclusion, suggesting a tripling over a two year period (1991/92-1993/94);

- A national estimate for the academic year 1993-94 indicates over 1,200 permanent exclusions of primary age children;

- The great majority of excluded children are boys;

- Physical aggression is the most common reason for all types of exclusion;

- Where evidence is available there is an over- representation of African-Caribbean boys in exclusion statistics;

- Case studies of children revealed some common characteristics in their home backgrounds, although it must be emphasised that there was a wide range of socio-economic circumstances:

  - a high incidence of family breakdown and relationship difficulties;

  - a high level of involvement of non-mainstream agencies with families (social services, child and family guidance, educational welfare, educational psychology, psychiatric services);

- a high proportion of the children were in receipt of statements of special education need or were in the process of formal assessment, almost always for Emotional and Behavioural difficulties;

- almost all parents and carers reported having difficulties with the children's behaviour out of school;

- most children did not enjoy being out of school and most could identify which behaviours led to their exclusion;

- there was no evidence that schools resort to permanent exclusion easily;

- most schools perceived they did not receive adequate support from the LEA or the multitude of other agencies with the most severe cases;

- fixed-term exclusion (usually a matter of days) is an indicator of major concern about a child's behaviour but its use may in part reflect a perceived lack of disciplinary options in some schools.

It is expected that the findings from this research will make a timely contribution to the debate and concerns about children with behavioural difficulties. By concentrating on younger children we hope to inform the development of preventative strategies and appropriate alternatives to mainstream education which may ultimately be more successful in retaining or returning children to mainstream education, than intervention occurring at a later age.

Title of the research project:
Exclusion From School and Alternatives
Date started: October 1994   **Completion date:** November 1996
Researcher(s): Pamela Munn; Gwynedd Lloyd; Margaret Johnstone; Mairi-Ann Cullen

Project aims:

- To map regional policy and practice;

- To explore head teacher perceptions of policy and practice;

- To analyse characteristics of excluded pupils;

- To explore in-school alternatives to exclusion;

- To gather perceptions of excluded pupils, their parents and others about the experiences of exclusion.

Research design:

- Analysis of regional policy documents;

- Telephone interviews with senior educational officials;

- Telephone interviews with a sample of 200 senior school staff;

- Interviews with teachers, pupils and others in 8 secondary and 4 primary schools.

Progress to date:

- Regional policy and procedures mapped and discussed;

- Telephone survey of schools completed;

- Case study work in secondary schools now in progress;

- Primary school case studies still to do.

What has been learned, or learned to date if the project is still in progress?

- Diversity of policy and practice across 12 regional and island authorities;

- General lack of awareness of policy aims at school level; an overwhelming concern with procedures;

- Use of informal exclusion even where this is officially banned;

- Importance of school culture in explaining variation in exclusion rates;

- Ranges of purposes of exclusion from part of hierarchy of sanctions in response to seemingly trivial offences to 'big bang' reaction.

Publications/reports available:

None as yet.

Name and address of person to contact for more information about this research:

Pamela Munn, Moray House Institute of Education, Holyrood Campus, Holyrood Road, Edinburgh EH8 8AQ

Title of research project:
ASSESSING SPECIAL EDUCATIONAL NEEDS
Date started: 1 April 1989   **Completion date:** 31 March 1991
Researcher(s): Derrick Armstrong, David Galloway, Sally Tomlinson

Project aims:
1. To elucidate the process of assessment from the perspectives of parents, children, professionals responsible for identifying special needs and administrators responsible for producing statements.

2. To describe, and provide a theoretical analysis of, sources of conflict and of agreement in the assessment process.

3. To develop a theoretical understanding of the concept of emotional and behavioural difficulties from the perspectives of the various people involved in assessment, whether as clients or as professionals.

Research design:
The research obtained case-study data on the assessment of 29 children identified by their teachers as having emotional and behavioural difficulties. The study population was drawn from 3 participating LEAs. We observed interviews related to the assessment, for example, between educational psychologists and parents, and psychologists and children. Subsequently we talked to each participant – professionals and clients – separately to elicit and discuss their perceptions of the purpose of each interview and what it had achieved.

Progress to date:
The research has now been completed.

What has been learned, or learned to date if the project is still in progress?
1. The purpose of assessment was seen as (a) securing the child's transfer to another school; or (b) provision of additional resources; or (c) provision of a 'safety net' if further problems were to occur in the future. The educational psychologists' contribution was largely reactive to this. Much of their work involved negotiations regarding the nature of the problem and the resources available in responding to it. Criteria for identifying EBD, independent of these considerations, seldom seemed to exist.

2. Parents frequently believed they had been given inadequate information about their own rights within the assessment procedures. Parents frequently felt themselves to be in a powerless position unable to influence professional decisions. A few parents did find ways of influencing the outcome of the assessment by actions they took outside of those procedures (e.g. changing their child's school).

3. There was evidence that some children saw the assessment as an explicit expectation that they would be 'naughty'. We found little evidence of children's views being sought by professionals. On the other hand, children's beliefs about the purpose of assessment could affect their behaviour in ways that professionals were unaware of.

Publications/reports available:

Galloway, D., S., and Armstrong, D., (1991) *Identifying Emotional and Behavioural Difficulties: Participant Perspectives* (Final Report to the Economic and Social Research Council, grant no. R000231393) Swindon: ESRC

Armstrong, D., (1995) *Power and Partnership in Education: Parents, Children and Special Educational Needs*, London: Routledge

Galloway, D., Armstrong, D., and Tomlinson, S., (1994) *The Assessment of Special Educational Needs: Whose Problem?* London: Longman

Name and address of person to contact for more information about this research:

Dr Derrick Armstrong, Division of Education, University of Sheffield, 388 Glossop Road, Sheffield S10 2JA

Title of the research project:

SCHOOL'S OUT:THE FAMILY PERSPECTIVE ON SCHOOL EXCLUSION

Date started: 1993   Completion date: 1994

Researcher(s): Ruth Cohan (Family Service Units), Mike Hughes (Barnardo's), Laura Ashworth (Advisory Centre on Education), Maud Blair (Open University, Swansea).

Aim:

To report on the perceptions of parents and pupils of the experience of being excluded from school, and to offer this insight as a contribution to the debate on school exclusion.

Research Design:

30 case studies of pupils who had been excluded from school were conducted by the research staff. More than half of these had been excluded permanently, others had been excluded indefinitely or for a fixed term. A small number had been excluded 'informally'.

Following this, 12 more detailed exploratory interviews were conducted, six with black families and six with white. The principal basis for selection was the families' willingness to talk about their experience.

Progress to date:

The study is completed, and written up in a joint publication by Barnardo's and Family Service Units' 'School's Out'.

What has been learnt:

The principle findings include:

1. **Types of Exclusion**

* Some pupils are being excluded repeatedly, and at some schools formal or informal exclusion is being used as a routine sanction rather than a last resort.

2. **The Home and the School**

* The families studied were often suffering from other stresses, including poverty, bad housing, illness or bereavement. In some instances such a home trauma triggered problems at school.

* Parents, though concerned about the difficulties experienced by their children often felt alienated from the school, looked down on by teachers, and powerless to influence how the school handled the situation of exclusion. This was particularly felt by parents of black children.

- Parents of children with behavioural and emotional difficulties often felt blamed for their children's behaviour.

3. **The School and the Pupil**

- Pupils were often out of school for long periods, with little or no educational input.

- Pupils with statements of special educational needs were being excluded from mainstream and special schools.

- Excluded pupils and their parents sometimes felt that they were excluded when they had been unfairly labelled as troublemakers.

- Most pupils interviewed wanted to be at school.

4. **Exclusion procedures**

- Some schools were reported not to have followed legal requirements for informing parents about exclusion.

- The lack of power experienced by parents was illustrated when negotiating with the school about the exclusion or other problems.

Publications/reports available:

Cohen, R., Hughes, M.J., Ashworth, L. and Blair, M., 1994, *School's Out: The Family Perspective on School Exclusion* Barnardo's and F.S.U.

Name and address of person to contact for more information about this research:

Dr. M.J. Hughes, Principle Officer Research and Development, Barnardo's, Policy and Development Unit, Tanners Lane, Barkingside, Ilford, Essex IG6 1QG

Title of research project:

SERVICES FOR CHILDREN AND YOUNG PEOPLE IN DIFFICULTY: CHANGING POLICIES, STRUCTURES AND PRACTICE

Date started: 1.2.95   **Completion Date:** 31.1.96

Researchers: Andrew Kendrick, Elizabeth Mapstone, Murray Simpson

Project Aims:

i) To give an account of developments which have taken place in Scotland in multi-professional and inter-organisational co-ordination of services for school age children in difficulty.

ii) to study current changes in health, social work, and education services and judicial provision which will affect collaboration in planning and service delivery for families and children.

iii) to identify potential problems and opportunities resulting from recent and proposed structural change and to highlight the emerging issues relevant to the provision of services for this group in the UK.

Research Design:

80 semi-structured interviews carried out at national and local level. At national level: representatives of central government, voluntary organisation, professional associations, consumer and user groups. In two geographical areas (greater Glasgow and Tayside Region) interviews at senior and middle management level with staff in: police, social work, education, reporter's departments and health agencies.

Progress to Date:

Fieldwork completed, analysis and write-up underway.

What has been learned, or learned to date if the project is still in progress:

There is a marked degree of uncertainty about the future of structures and mechanisms of inter-disciplinary working beyond April 1996. Concerns have been expressed regarding a number of issues as they impact on joint working:

resources
boundary issues
specialisation
differing structures of management
issues of scale
purchaser/provider split
decentralisation and local autonomy

It is considered that the smaller, unitary authorities will provide the opportunity for a greater corporate identity, particularly affecting education and social work. The statutory duty set out in the Children (Scotland) Act to produce

Children's Services plans is thought to provide an important opportunity to promote inter-disciplinary working.

Publications/reports available

Soon, hopefully!!!

Contact Person

Andrew Kendrick, Department of Social Work, University of Dundee, Dundee DD1 4HN

Tel: 01382 344739, Fax: 01382 221512,

email: a.j.kendrick@dundee.ac.uk

Murray Simpson, Department of Social Work, University of Dundee, Dundee DD1 4HN

Tel: 01382 344948, Fax: 01382 221512,

email: m.k.simpson@dundee.ac.uk

Title of research project:
RESIDENTIAL CARE IN THE INTEGRATION OF CHILD CARE SERVICES
Date started: 1.3.89   **Completion Date:** 30.9.94
Researchers: Andrew Kendrick, Elizabeth Mapstone, Anne Mollison, Susan Busby, Sandy Fraser.

Project Aims:

To provide information on placement outcomes for 250 children in care in three Scottish Social Work Departments over a period of three years.

To provide detailed information of the use and appropriateness of residential child care resources and relate this to outcomes through evaluation of identified elements of child care provision.

To examine the factors which promote integration of child care services including inter-agency relationships, particularly social work and education.

Research Design:

Outcome study of 200 children in the care of three local authority Social Work Departments. Children identified at reception into care or at change in placement. Primary source of information was interviews with the child's social worker. In order to provide information on different perspectives and expectations of placement outcomes, sub-sample of 30 children and young people were identified and interviews carried out with involved professionals, foster parents, parents and young people themselves.

Three linked studies were made of services incorporating specific features of 'integrated child care': residential outreach work; a centre for young people; and a multi-agency strategy for young people. The latter involved interviews with key professionals; questionnaires to individuals actively involved in local strategy groups; and analysis of minutes of multi-disciplinary case conferences and other decision-making meetings.

Progress to date:
Completed.

What has been learned, or learned to date if the project is still in progress.

Children in local authority care suffer from a number of educational disadvantages. Partly, this is due to the high level of disruption caused by movement between care placements which often involves a change of school. Almost half of the children and young people in mainstream education were reported to have had problems of non-attendance at school before they were received into care. Almost three-fifths of the school age children changed school or alternative educational provision, either at admission to care or during the twelve months; one in ten changed three or more times.

Where children in the study were in alternative day educational provision, social workers were very positive about the contribution it made.

One-fifth of the residential placements in the study were in residential schools. The benefits of residential schooling in terms of education were stressed. Often after months, or even years, where young people had not been receiving education, residential schools were providing the environment in which they could achieve some degree of educational success. Residential schooling is expensive, however, and the relationship between social work and education could be fraught when it came to the question of payment for the placement.

Recent years have seen a number of initiatives in Scotland with the intention of creating more 'systematic case co-ordination' between social work, education and other agencies. Some have been explicitly related to keeping children out of residential schooling and developing a range of community-based resources to support children whose needs were not being met in mainstream education. Others have been based on a broader 'community development' approach.

In one recently established youth strategy, local groups have developed in various ways. In some areas, the consultation of young people has been given highest priority and various consultation exercises to find out what young people wanted was carried out. The setting up of youth information services, led by community education, has been an important contribution to the strategy. The sharing of information and ideas between professionals and community groups was highlighted as a success by participants in the strategy.

Publications/reports available

Kendrick, A. (1995) *Residential Care in the Integration of Child Care Services*, Central Research Unit Papers, The Scottish Office, Edinburgh.

Kendrick, A. (1995) 'Supporting Families Through Inter-Agency Work: Youth Strategies in Scotland', in M. Hill, R. Kirk and D. Part (eds) *Supporting Families*, Edinburgh: HMSO, pp. 135 – 148.

Kendrick, A. (1995) 'The Integration of Child Care Services in Scotland', *Children and Youth Services Review*, Vol 17, No 5 – 6, pp. 619 – 635.

Contact Person

Andrew Kendrick, Department of Social Work, University of Dundee, Dundee DD1 4HN

Tel: 01382 344739, Fax: 01383 221512

email: a.j.kendrick@dundee.ac.uk

Title of research project:

AN EVALUATION OF NCH ACTION FOR CHILDREN PERTH AND KINROSS RURAL YOUTH PROJECT

Date started: 1.12.93   **Completion Date:** 30.9.94

Researchers: Andrew Kendrick

Project Aims:

i)   perceptions of professionals in other agencies of the project's effectiveness;

ii) feedback from young people and their parents on their involvement in the project; and

iii) outcomes in relation to a sample of young people with whom the Project had worked.

Research Design:

Case profiles of 50 young people involved with the project; questionnaires to 50 young people involved with the project and to their parents; a small number of interviews with young people; telephone interviews with 18 staff of other agencies, interviews with project staff.

Progress to Date:

Completed.

What has been learned to date if the project is still in progress

Educational problems can quickly escalate in rural areas as exclusion from one school creates major difficulties in finding a place in another distant school. The project offers groupwork and/or individual work to young people in order to maintain them within their families, communities and mainstream education. School-based groups have been run for pupils presenting difficulties in school. Between 1991 and 1993, two-thirds of referrals came from social work, one fifth from schools, and smaller numbers from Educational Support Service and Educational Psychology. The project (unlike others run by NCH) is not jointly funded by the education department and since fieldwork for the evaluation was competed, the project has been increasingly unable to take on referrals from schools because of the increase in the number and complexity of social work cases. In the sample children, exactly half the referrals involved behaviour problems at school and one fifth attendance problems. Overall, involvement with the project was considered to have had a positive effect for two-thirds of young people they worked with. Good working relationships had been established with other agencies, particularly the schools and education staff.

Publications/reports available

Kendrick, A. (1994) *An Evaluation of NCH Action for Children Perth and Kinross Rural Youth Project*, University of Dundee Department of Social Work.

Kendrick, A. and Rioch, C. (forthcoming) 'Knowing the Back Roads: Rural Social Work with Troubled Young People', *Youth & Policy*.

Contact Person

Andrew Kendrick, Department of Social Work, University of Dundee, Dundee DD1 4HN

Tel: 01382 344739, Fax: 01382 221512
email: a.j.kendrick@dundee.ac.uk

Title of the research project:

THE EXCLUSION FROM SCHOOL OF CHILDREN LOOKED AFTER BY LOCAL AUTHORITIES IN RESIDENTIAL ACCOMMODATION

Date started: June 1994   **Completion date:** 1997

Researchers: Isabelle Brodie (Research Assistant, University of Luton), David Berridge (Professor of Child and Family Welfare, University of Luton).

Project aims:

To investigate:

- the interactions between, and the views of, the different individuals engaged in the exclusion process – young people, teachers, head teachers, social workers, parents, educational psychologists and educational welfare officers.

- the factors which contribute to an exclusion taking place and influence the way in which it is experienced, including liaison between services.

- the way in which exclusion operates in the light of current legislation and guidance relating to the educational welfare of children looked after.

Research design:

The research is being carried out in association with a study of children's homes in three local authorities, two of which are participating in the exclusions research. Ten cases of permanent exclusion are being identified via children's homes in each authority. Cases include children of both primary and secondary school age. Interviews are then carried out with the range of individuals involved in the exclusion process – residential staff, teachers, head teachers, young people, social workers parents, educational welfare officers and educational psychologists. Case files are also examined.

Progress to date:

Fieldwork for the study commenced in March 1995. In one local authority, five cases of permanent exclusion among secondary school age children have been identified and the first phase of data collection completed. Work has begun on a further three cases of primary school exclusion. Negotiations have been completed with the second authority and four cases already identified.

What has been learned, or learned to date if the project is still in progress?

- While only a small number of cases have been examined so far, it appears that exclusion tends to follow a serious incident preceded by a build-up of tension. It is usually considered to be justified by young people, residential staff and teachers. Permanent exclusion often occurs prior to entry to the children's home. This suggests that, rather than the young person's looked after status leading to exclusion, children's homes are often more involved in addressing extreme, pre-existing educational difficulties.

- The young people interviewed typically disliked school and sometimes claimed to have manipulated exclusion. They appear to have poor social networks at school and this in turn heightened the appeal of increased contact with the peer group at the children's homes.

- Head teachers were very conscious of the pressures resulting from limited resources and an inflexible curriculum when dealing with pupils displaying educational difficulties.

- Schools feel that Social Services has little understanding of school organisation and processes. There is also a continuing sense of difference in culture and philosophy.

- Residential staff are often unsure whether a young person is excluded or is a non-attender. Consequently effective action may not always be taken in response to an exclusion, e.g. an appeal. Generally the involvement of residential staff in schooling tended to be limited to 'crisis management'.

- The allocation of Social Services roles regarding the education of children looked after is not always clear and responsibilities are not always defined.

- Education is not automatically prioritised by Social Services and social workers do not always act strategically in situations where it is clear an educational placement is tenuous. Where a social worker is especially proactive, this tends to be viewed as an individual commitment, leading to considerable variability in the way in which schooling is addressed.

Publications/reports available:

Brodie, I. (1995) *Highlight: Exclusion From School*. London: National Children's Bureau.

Berridge, D. and Brodie, I. (1996) 'Residential child care in England and Wales: the enquiries and after', in Hill, M. and Aldgate, J. (eds) *Child Welfare Services: Developments in Law, Policy, Practice and Research*. London: Jessica Kingsley.

Name and address of person to contact for more information about the research:

Isabelle Brodie, Department of Professional Social Studies,
Park Square, Luton LU1 3JU
Tel: 01582-32886
email: Isabelle.Brodie@luton.ac.uk

Title of Project:

OUTCAST ENGLAND: HOW SCHOOLS EXCLUDE BLACK CHILDREN

Date Started: 1993   **Completion Date:** 1994 but continuing to monitor

Researchers: Jenny Bourne, Lee Bridges, and Chris Searle,

Project Aims:

The Institute of Race Relations (IRR) serves as a 'think tank' on issues of racism, particularly as they affect those in the black community who suffer from its various impacts in their daily lives. It monitors various aspects of racism and produces periodic information and analyses of these, in the form of resource materials, bulletins, booklets and pamphlets.

In 1993 the IRR decided to produce a booklet analysing the issue of rising school exclusions from the perspective of racism and racial justice. Funding to support work on this booklet and its publication was given by the Gulbenkian Foundation. The aim was not so much to conduct academic research on exclusions as to bring together the various sources of information about their impact on black pupils and the wider black community; to set this information in a historical context relating to the development of both educational policy and race relations: and to put forward recommendations that might form the basis for action (as distinct from further research) by and for the black community on the issue of school exclusions.

Research design:

The booklet sets out to examine the issue of race and exclusions from three distinct perspectives. First, it has been set in the context of the wider development of educational policy from the 1960s onwards, with particular focus on the post-1988 reforms, and of the historic failure of the British school system to address the needs of the black community. Secondly, the issue of exclusions is examined from the perspective of a (now former) head teacher of an inner city school who has adopted a policy against exclusions, in the face of stiff opposition from many teachers, their trade unions, and local and central authorities. Thirdly, the impact of exclusions on black pupils and their parents is analysed through a review of statistical and other research information and by a series of case studies illustrating different aspects of the problem.

Progress to date:

The booklet *Outcast England: How Schools Exclude Black Children*, was published early in 1994. Since then, the IRR has participated in various discussions, particularly through the Commission on Racial Equality, about how policy on exclusions can be addressed from the perspective of its racial impact. There has been little progress in terms of action on this issue from official bodies, either centrally or locally, although there continue to be very active campaigns around the issue among black community groups in different parts of the country, frequently with little or no financial or other support from local authorities or schools. None of the recommendations set out in the booklet have been addressed, let alone implemented. To the contrary, since publication of the 'Pupils with Problems' Circulars in 1994, official policy has moved in a more reactionary direction, under pressure from the various teachers' unions.

What has been learned from the project?

A specific lesson of this project (and others carried out by the Institute of Race Relations over the years) is that research which is directed primarily at policy-makers (let alone more academic studies), no matter how well- intentioned, is unlikely to have a beneficial effect in terms of changing the direction of policy. To the extent that further 'research' on exclusions is justified, it needs to be focused on the needs of those who are at the sharp end of the problem – black pupils, their parents and communities – and specifically designed to assist them in their struggles and campaigns around the issue. In this respect, it may be suggested that two issues of concern are (i) the working and reform of exclusion procedures and appeals and the need to provide support for children and parents in the process; (ii) giving children, parents and communities 'rights' in relation to the provision of education 'otherwise than at school'.

Publications available:

Bourne, Jenny, Bridges, Lee, and Searle, Chris, *Outcast England: How Schools Exclude Black Children* available from Institute of Race Relations, 2–6 Leeke Street, London WC1X 9HS Tel. 0171-837-0041 (price £3 plus 50p postage)

Title of the research project:

GOVERNMENT POLICY AND EXCLUSIONS FROM SCHOOL

Date started: 1988 ERA and EBD. Master of Education thesis, Westminster College Oxford. Submitted 1991.

1991 Government Policy and Exclusions from School. PhD thesis, University of Warwick. Completion date: 1996.

Researcher: Margaret Stirling. 1990-1995 employed as Advisory teacher by the Social Services Department Birmingham. This role entailed ensuring the educational entitlement of children looked after by the local authority.

Project aims:

To conduct a policy study, primarily with ethnographic research, within a metropolitan authority; in order to consider the relationship between educational policy and exclusion practices.

Research Design:

The research sets out to examine: (i) Patterns of Exclusion, (ii) States of Exclusion, and (iii) Provision for Excluded pupils; and to consider the significance of the exclusion process in terms of education policy.

The theoretical model employed in examining the effect of policy, is to identify dominant discourses, (for example entitlement to 'choice and diversity'), and to contextualise the research findings in respect of these discourses, in order to examine their validity. Prevailing discursive themes run as longitudinal 'strands' throughout the chapters of the thesis, which follow the exclusion 'tariff'.

The research draws on a hundred in-depth semi-structured interviews with key professionals in the field, conducted over a research period of six years. It also draws on extensive background data from referrals to the Social Services in the city authority, including three hundred detailed case files, working during the past few years.

Progress to date:

The field research is complete. The thesis is presently being written up for submission in the Autumn.

What has been learned, or learned to date if the project is still in progress?

Early research 1988-1991, showed a rise in exclusions from school. Current research, 1991-1995 examines the effect of government education policy in practice on school exclusions; showing a rise in unofficial exclusions and pupils with minimal education for unacceptable periods. The thesis considers exclusion trends to be largely policy dependent; it examines the practical effects of policy in terms of whom it empowers or disempowers and views exclusion as a continuum of marginalisation. Central to the argument is the concept of exclusion as a process of disempowerment.

Predominant policy discourses are considered in the light of the field research. In respect of 'Choice' and 'Diversity' in education, evidence is presented which shows a stratified education system, one in which market forces control access to a hierarchy of schools reinforcing social class differences, rather than max-imising educational potential and creating opportunities for social mobility.

The research proposes that diversity, or disparity, is necessary in the competi-tive operation of market forces which control access to a hierarchical system of schools, ensuring existing class differentials; and that equality of educational opportunity is incompatible with values invested in a differentiated education system.

Publications/reports available:

SPECIAL CHILDREN Absent with Leave. November 1991

MANAGING SCHOOLS TODAY The Exclusion Zone. November 1991

YOUNG MINDS Journal of The National Association for Child and Family Mental Health. The Education Reform Act and EBD children. March 1992

THE TIMES EDUCATIONAL SUPPLEMENT Squeezed out of a Combative World. 26 June 1992

BRITISH JOURNAL OF SPECIAL EDUCATION How Many Pupils Are Being Excluded? December 1992

SPECIAL CHILDREN Second Classes for a Second Class? May 1993

PERSPECTIVE The Journal for Advisors and Inspectors. Diversity or Division? July 1993

MULTICULTURAL EDUCATION REVIEW A 'Black Mark' Against Him? December 1993

MULTICULTURAL EDUCATION REVIEW Two London Conferences on Pupil Exclusions. December 1993

SPECIAL CHILDREN The End Of The Line: Special School Exclusions. June 1994

and Chapter Four in a forthcoming book:

Stirling M (1996) Government Policy and Disadvantaged Children. Ed. E Blyth, J Milner *School Exclusions: Inter Professional Issues for Policy and Practice.* Routledge.

Name and address of person to contact for more information about this research:

Margaret Stirling, Head Teacher, Underley Hall School, Kirkby Lonsdale, Carnforth, Lancashire LA 2HE

Title of the research project:
A STUDY OF THE CULTURE OF SCHOOL-LESSNESS

Date started: September 1994   **Completion date:** Ongoing longitudinal study

Researchers: Professor Mary John; Dr Bill Taylor; Dr Vanessa Parffrey and Gordon Jack

Project aims:
To establish what children at three stages in their school-life do all day when not attending school – for reason of exclusion/voluntary non-attendance through circumstances such as disability, hospitalisation, family movement/travels, frequently changing places of residence. In essence we are looking at the culture of school-lessness and what, if any, its educational advantages/disadvantages are (cf John, 1996, in press).

Research design:
An accelerated longitudinal design using 4 'cross-sections' – one pre-school, one 5-7, one 7-11, one 14+. The method of enquiry involves both quantitative and qualitative methods, peer interviewing, shadowing and a semiotic method.

Progress to date:

- We have completed pilot studies of young children living in temporary accommodation and at family centres (John and Still, 1993, unpublished).

- We have completed a pilot project of children in school exclusion units (Parffrey, 1994).

- Preliminary work with various groups of young people in the age range towards the end of compulsory schooling has begun.

- We have undertaken a detailed trawl of the country (Eastern Region) statistics for school exclusion.

- We have been supported by the county council in a meeting for data collection and networking with 25 head teachers and senior advisors and educational psychologists.

- Likewise a meeting with all social services and voluntary agencies involved in any work with children out of school.

- We have continued our liaison work with all the agencies listed on the attached outline.

What has been learned, or learned to date if the project is still in progress?
Still in progress but:

- How difficult it is to access young people out of school.

- How uncoordinated (and underfunded) are the agencies concerned with 'homeless' children and young people.

- How the young people, staff and educational psychologists feel about exclusion (Parffrey,1994).

- How much in breach of the child's right to an education (Articles 26? and 29) of the UN Convention of the Rights of the Child we are at the present time.

Publications/reports available:

Parffrey, V. (1994) "Exclusion: failed children or systems failure?', *School Organisation*, 14,2,107-120.

John, M. (1993) 'Children with Special Needs as the Casualties of a Free Market Economy', *International Journal of Children's Rights*, vol.11,1-31.

John, M. (1996 forthcoming) 'Monitoring Children's Rights to Education in the South West of England', in , E. *Monitoring Children's Rights*, Dordrecht: Martinus Nijholt.

Name and address of person to contact for more information about this research:

Professor Mary John, Dean of the Faculty of Education, School of Education, University of Exeter, St Lukes, Heavitree Road, Exeter EX1 2LU

Tel: 01392-264772

Title of the research project:
SHEFFIELD SCHOOL AND HOME PROJECT
Date started: January 1978   **Completion date:** December 1979
Researcher(s): David Galloway, Tina Ball, Diana Blomfield, Rosalind Seyd

Project aims: To establish the prevalence of, and reasons for, exclusion in schools in Sheffield LEA.

Research design:
1. Statistical analysis of all exclusions in a four year period;
2. Intensive study of all pupils excluded for more than three weeks in a one year period.
3. Analysis of school variables associated with exclusion.

Progress to date:
Completed 1979.

What has been learned, or learned to date if the project is still in progress?
Pupils who are excluded long term or indefinitely constitute an *exceptionally* vulnerable group on cognitive, medical and social criteria.

In spite of the multiple vulnerability of these pupils, the dominant influence on whether or not they are excluded is the school they happen to be attending.

The factors associated with the school's influence on exclusion are not the same as those associated with the school's equally great influence on behaviour within the classroom.

Consistent features of schools with low exclusion rates are: senior staff support their colleagues but do not remove responsibility from them; serious disciplinary incidents are dealt with decisively in their own right, but are also seen as evidence of the need to review aspects of the school's provision for the curriculum, pastoral care and special educational needs; the dominant policy is inclusive rather than exclusive; consequently, there is no attempt to draw spurious distinctions between pupils who are 'disturbed' and pupils who are 'disruptive'.

Publications/reports available:
Galloway, D., Ball, T., Blomfield, D. and Seyd, R. (1982) *Schools and Disruptive Pupils.* London: Longman.
Galloway, D. (1995) 'Truancy, Delinquency, Disruption and Exclusion: Differential School Influences?', *British Psychological Society Education Sector Review*, 19,2,49-60.

Name and address of person to contact for more information about this research:
Professor David Galloway, School of Education, University of Durham, Leazes Road, Durham DH1 1TA